For

A GARDEN
OF
ONE'S OWN

EDITED AND COMPILED BY
Solomon M. Skolnick and Marc Anello

ILLUSTRATIONS BY
Carol Eldridge

PETER PAUPER PRESS, INC.
WHITE PLAINS, NEW YORK

Copyright © 1996
Peter Pauper Press, Inc.
202 Mamaroneck Avenue
White Plains, NY 10601
ISBN 0-88088-795-8

Book design by Susan Hood

Printed in Hong Kong
7 6 5 4 3 2 1

INTRODUCTION

A garden is a cherished living thing. It can be a sanctuary, or a place for family gatherings; a plot run riot with the scent of flowers, or a magnet for the alighting of birds. To dig, to plant, to simply marvel at the flowers or to pinch them back, the myriad tasks of the garden have the power to engage us, or let our minds run free. Our personalities mingle with that of the garden. It is a growing place, a place which, if we apply the proper respect for the natural motion of all things, we can, for a time, call our own.

S. M. S.

Gardening is a lifelong adventure.

Nancy Bubel

The visionary may find that some haunting garden of an inner dream shapes all the gardens of his future.

Ann Lovejoy

I am a wayward, willful, contrary gardener. I don't follow seed-packet directions.

Barbara Dodge Borland

It is utterly forbidden to be half-hearted about gardening. You have got to love your garden whether you like it or not.

W. C. Sellar and R. J. Yeatman

An exercise in faith, it has been called, this consumptive pastime of ours; to believe that a bed, once more colorful with handwritten plastic than plants, would become a billowing border the following spring.

Daniel Hinkley and Robert Jones

Gardening is about remembering what has been done, what needs doing, what things look like, and when flowers bloom. While every year I forget to send birthday cards, I can remember to divide the meadow rue and the painted ferns. My own garden memories are part of a tradition . . .

Ferris Cook

In childhood a dollar did not mean a hundred cents, but twenty packets of flower-seeds; ten cents, a clump of pansies, a verbena, or a small geranium; while twenty-five cents stood for a heliotrope, a Fuchsia, or a tearose in forced and consequently hectic bloom.

Mabel Osgood Wright

I think the reason that Grandmama's garden is so well remembered is that children were allowed to pick as many flowers as they needed, for there was nothing rare or choice in the flower beds: petunias, four-o'clocks, roses—the more they were picked, the better they bloomed.

Elizabeth Lawrence

I learned about gardening soon after I learned to walk. Tagging after my grandpa with my little watering can, I sprinkled where he hosed, jabbed at the earth with my toy shovel where he cultivated the soil, peered at the flowers that he examined.

Ruth Shaw Ernst

FRESH FROM THE GARDEN

My garden is a veritable album, and as I wander over our place I find many a dear friend or happy hour commemorated in it.

Mrs. Theodore Thomas

A herb garden needs no window dressing from other brilliant flowers—herb foliage makes a varied and harmonious tapestry of leaves, and its gentle flowers are a bonus. Above all, of course, there are the scents—crushed in your fingers they linger, and as you walk by they waft towards you in a tantalising medley.

Rosemary Verey

Gardeners, like plants, invariably grow from small beginnings.

Geraldene Holt

The love of gardening is a seed that once sown never dies.

Gertrude Jekyll

Seedsmen reckon that their stock in trade is not seeds at all . . . it's optimism. That's what they're selling when you're seduced by that gorgeous picture on the front of the packet.

Geoff Hamilton

Some flowers are so relentlessly happy-looking that it is hard to appreciate them when you are in a sullen mood.

Mary Forsell

No occupation is so delightful to me as the culture of the earth and no culture comparable to that of the garden.

Thomas Jefferson

Garden makers in history have been intent on creating earthly paradises.

Michael Laurie

The snow lies on the ground, patchily, not with a good warm covering, but like a tattered shawl that lets in the cold. I know just where to look for the newcomers in the borders when spring calls them out.

Helen Ashe Hayes

Anticipation is one of the joys of gardening and if you know how and where to look you can find signs of each season long before the calendar confirms it.

Nancy Goodwin

A natural garden . . . includes the wide, wild world as it is, warts and all.

Jeff Cox

[The garden is] a refuge, a place of quiet contemplation, a source of nourishment for mind and body alike.

Dean Pailler

Gardening is such a mixture of mistakes and successes, and I often think the mistakes are the most important.

Barbara Dodge Borland

Each within his green inclosure is a creator, and no two shall reach the same conclusion . . .

Louise Beebe Wilder

We know enough of the internal workings of the seed to stand in awe at its variety, its toughness, and its practical simplicity.

Nancy Bubel

It is difficult to imagine a world without roses.

Peter Beales

The rose laughs at my long-looking, my constantly wondering what a *rose* means, and who *owns* the rose, whatever it means.

Jeláluddin Rumi

GROW MIX

5 lbs.

The rose is ordinary ornamental, grown in every garden—and extraordinary image, glowing in the mind.

Ram and Marissa Fishman

This is a garden you can meander through for hours. Pillars to the right and left are laden with rosebuds, and the breezes, when they stir, carry the blossoms' perfume on their breath.

Tovah Martin

The columbines, stone blue, or deep
    night brown,
Their honey-comb like blossoms
    hanging down;
Each cottage garden's fond adopted
    child,
Though heaths still claim them,
    where they yet grow wild.

John Clare

The ivory bugles blow scent instead
of sound.

Samuel Pepys

To grow daylilies is to love them. And to love them is to want as many different varieties as possible. . . . So beware! If you are susceptible to their attractions, daylilies can rule your garden and, sometimes, your life.

Sydney Eddison

Black Sage—One must wonder where these common names come from; although the leaves on this native are a deep, glossy green, they certainly could not be mistaken for black. Nor the flowers; they're lavender blue!

Flowery Branch Seed Co.

Even the most ordinary plants will take on a new significance if you will refuse the associations that spring to mind and try to see their form, texture and colour as though for the first time.

Russell Page

When I began to dig and plant, I little knew the joy which would grow out of the soil, and descend from the skies, and gather from far-off places and times to gladden my soul . . .

Candace Wheeler

Most of the herbs we grow in our garden are perennials—which means they reappear each year as if by magic . . .

Barbara Milo Ohrbach

You don't know the luxury of grass underfoot until you've been on stone for six weeks. It's worth all the labor and all the fuss, even if it has weeds in it. If you want to learn to love a dandelion, try going without one for a bit.

Janet Gillespie

Your garden is a place as favorable to plant and animal life as it is pleasing to the human eye . . . and nose, for the myriad sweet scents; and ear, for the chatter of birds; and mouth, for the harvest-fresh flavors of berries and vegetables; and hands, for the velvety feel of the petals of a pansy or wild poppy.

Ruth Shaw Ernst

All morning in the garden. . . . Em says that I look like a mad man. What have I done to look that way? Merely hunted insects on my rosebushes.

André Gide

Behold the earth appareled with plants—as with a robe of embroidered work.

John Gerard

The strongest, most productive garden implement you can ever obtain probably won't be for sale in tool catalogs or implement stores; you won't find it listed in seed catalogs or stocked in your favorite garden center. Yet this tool is far mightier than the hoe; it will dig deeper than a tiller and will lay off rows better than any wheel planter. It's the most valuable implement a gardener can ever use: a pencil.

Jim Long

A friend described the backyard as a secret garden—a private place to call one's own.

Richard Saunders

To flower and plant and tree, the garden is a cloistered refuge from the battle of life.

Frances Bardswell

No matter how long you've been gardening, there is something surprising about seeing a butterfly... Frail, unexpected, temporary. A butterfly always seems on its way somewhere else.

Kevin Pearce

A garden gives you back what you
put into it.

Thalassa Cruso

For myself, I like having flowers to smell when I walk in the garden, flowers to cut for the house, flowers to share with friends. Having these in abundance proves the methods of my madness to be working well, and well worthwhile.

Susan Urshel

Not a gardener has crossed my path whose work or advice has not in some way enriched me, and each encounter has created an indelible bond of friendship, of experience shared.

Pamela Jones

To get things off to a good start, one qualification for life membership in the gardening fraternity is banishment of the word "dirt." The substance you dig and plant in—the good earth—is called "soil." Dirt is what you wash off your face.

Joan Lee Faust

Digging in the dirt under the heat of a midsummer sun can provide a gardener with earthly delights, but such work also is tough on skin and nails.

Country Home's Country Gardens Magazine

It is such earthy work: The rich smell of living soil, the feel of it sifting through the fingers, the strength of it when filled with roots, the promise of it when open for planting.

Monica Moran Brandies

Until a man has known this rhythm of spading, he knows not gardening. It is the first essential. All other acts that gardening entails cannot compare with this one simple process in profound necessity. Profound because it is changeless and simple as all time-aged customs come to be . . .

Richardson Wright

Some people call this a cottage garden, but it's just a good messy garden. There's no plan. It's not like painting—I just stick the plants in. I like large quantities of blooms all jumbled together.

Tasha Tudor

To a lover of roses, no spot affords more contentment, more pleasure or more encouragement than his rose garden. . . . Its serenity smoothes wrinkles from the mind and freshens it for greater endeavor. Its care provides a healthful physical antidote for all mental vapors.

Arthur F. Truex

Someone once said of a beautiful public garden, "It just shows what God could do if He had the money." But even the grubbiest garden, abounding with weeds, shows what we can do without money just because God is so good.

Monica Moran Brandies

It should be clearly understood that gardening is not something that can be hurried along to meet one's requirements. Nature *must* take Her course.

Madeline Dolowich

Reading the flower lists is like reading poetry, for the flowers are called by their sweet country names, many of them belonging to Shakespeare and the Bible.

Elizabeth Lawrence

If one orders a plant catalogued as "rose coloured," it is sure to arrive that dear besmirched hue—magenta. I have no quarrel with magenta, but I do not want it when my heart is set upon a delightful pink, and some spot in my garden is especially designed to hold it.

Louise Beebe Wilder

From all this peril here at last set
  free,
In the garden all find security.

>   Ode to a Garden Carpet,
>   *by an unknown Sufi poet,*
>   *c. 1500*

What was Paradise?
   But a Garden.
an orchard of trees
   and Herbs
Full of pleasure, and
   Nothing there but Delights.

William Lawson,
17th c.

A real gardener is not a man who cultivates flowers; he is a man who cultivates the soil . . . If he came into the Garden of Eden he would sniff excitedly and say: "Good Lord, what humus!"

Karel Čapek

At bulb-planting time, it is always an effort to bury all one's wealth in the ground. . . . Well, maybe just *one* pot for forcing.

Joe Eck and Wayne Winterrowd

When in these fresh mornings I go into my garden before anyone is awake, I go for the time being into perfect happiness. In this hour divinely fresh and still, the fair face of every flower salutes me with a silent joy that fills me with infinite content; each gives me its color, its grace, its perfume, and enriches me with the consummation of its beauty.

Celia Thaxter

The work of a garden bears visible fruits—in a world where most of our labours seem suspiciously meaningless.

Pam Brown

Gardeners are generous because nature is generous to them.

Elizabeth Lawrence

When you pour a packet of seeds into your hand and begin to place them the proper distance apart in the furrow, you become not just a participant, but a custodian of life.

D. Landreth Seed
Company Catalog

Seeds are a link to the past.

Rosalind Creasy

Get a garden!

Walafrid Strabo